"Joanna has written an incredi
rising stars, equipping and em   n
to the fullest. This is a fun and
all ages!"

CALLEDOUT MUSIC, international gospel artist and songwriter

"I wish this book had been available for me! I know this will inspire my kids' faith - it's real and practical, fun and engaging. The content is so helpful for primary-schoolers who want to know Jesus better every day. I highly recommend it."

ABBY GUINNESS, head of Spring Harvest

"I feel as though I've personally prayed this book into being! It is so necessary, now more than ever. We are the only Bibles some of the young people in our worlds will ever read. And what Joanna has done here is SUCH a great representation of her fun, funky approach to knowing Jesus. Buy at least ten copies just to give away!"

CHIP KENDALL, worship artist and presenter

"This lively and beautifully written set of devotions, based largely on Joanna's own childhood experiences, will surely help the children in your life grow closer to the God who made and loves them."

BOB HARTMAN, author and performance storyteller

"Joanna is everyone's best champion and cheerleader! This jampacked, heartfelt, creative book is exactly what I needed as a young person - and even as an adult now!"

MARTHA SHRIMPTON, founder of Nimbus Collective and author of *Wow! Jesus*

"I defy anyone to not have their hope raised by this fun-tastic devotional. Its pages are dripping with wisdom, truth, and joy. It's the antidote to many of cultures' prevalent messages, and will cause faith to arise in the heart of every young reader!

Joanna is a joy-carrier, the overflow of her day-by-day walk with the Spirit. The pages of this book are like moments with her, leading the reader to raise their eyes heavenward."

DAVE HILL, Bethel Kids Director and HeartSmart founder

"Joanna knows just what children need from a devotional. She has drawn upon her own faith experience to collate a wonderful selection of relatable personal experiences, Bible verses, and creative ways to process thoughts and feelings. This is an ideal devotional to develop faith through journalling and to prepare young hearts for the future."

GEMMA HUNT, TV presenter and author

"It can be hard to find books for 7–11s that are faith-filled but also really fun and engaging. *What's Up* ticks all the boxes. Joanna's warm writing style teamed with the lively illustrations will pull young readers in and help them to question, challenge, and build their faith without even realizing they're doing it. With contributions from other awe-inspiring Christians, it's a great way to open up dialogue around issues such as fear, friendship, grief, and anger. A must-read for the pre-teens in our families and churches."

DEBRA GREEN OBE, executive director, Redeeming Our Communities

"Finally a book we want our kids to read. Joanna has such a gift for communicating to the younger generation. She understands what grabs their attention and will get them to stop, listen, and think! This devotional-style book is written in a way that helps make the truth of God's word and character relatable to kids, and will help them understand how to apply it to everyday life. Packed with wisdom and fun, it will help to equip our kids for some of the challenges of the world we live in today."

JAY AND ZOË COOK, worship leaders and pastors at Hillsong Southwest London

"*What's Up* is a must-read devotional book. Perfectly pitched, Joanna hits relevant and meaningful topics for the age group, and isn't afraid to use her own experiences to explore an array of issues – from friendship to grief. We will definitely be recommending this fantastic book to our Virtual Sunday Schoolers!"

ROB AND NAT HOLMAN, founders of Virtual Sunday School and 4Front Theatre Company

"*What's Up* is a light for young hearts, illuminating their path with timeless wisdom, grace, empathy, and emotional intelligence. It speaks directly to their hearts! Joanna Adeyinka-Burford's words are both a comfort and a challenge, inspiring our children to grow and thrive. This book is a must-have for every young soul navigating their journey of faith."

YOLANDA BROWN OBE DL, musician and broadcaster

"Children need voices like Joanna's to offer sound wisdom, a non-judgemental perspective, and a faith-filled reminder of the thing that's most important: Jesus. *What's Up* is the ideal companion to a young person in the process of making their parents' faith their own or starting to learn about God from scratch. The bite-sized encouragements are an accessible and wise reminder to kids that we should always 'look up', no matter 'what's up'."

LAUREN WINDLE, author, presenter and public speaker

"Joanna has not only crafted a wonderful book, but also a heartfelt message that resonates with a young audience. Her genuine heart for young people shines through every page. This book serves as a fantastic resource, fostering self-confidence in children through interactive elements that provide practical tools for personal growth. But what really sets this book apart is its beautiful integration of God's love. Joanna skillfully weaves a narrative showcasing unconditional love, encouraging children to embrace and radiate that love in their lives. I highly recommend Joanna's book to parents, caregivers, and anyone looking to inspire the young hearts around them."

CHARLIE BLYTHE, Europe Regional Director, A21

This book is dedicated to
Nathaniel & Taiya xxx

What's Up
30 encouragements to fuel your faith
Joanna Adeyinka-Burford

STARSHINE B★OKS

Published by **Starshine Books**
Part of the SPCK Group
Society for Promoting Christian Knowledge
The Record Hall, 16–16A Baldwins Gardens
London EC1N 7RJ
www.spck.org.uk

Paperback ISBN 978-1-91574-901-7
ebook ISBN 978-1-91574-902-4
Audiobook ISBN 978-1-91574-903-1

Acknowledgements
The publisher would like to thank Rhys Stephenson, Emma Borquaye, Tracy
Wood, and Pete Sheath for their contributions.

Scripture quotations marked 'ICB' are from the Holy Bible, International
Children's Bible® Copyright© 1986, 1988, 1999, 2015 by Thomas Nelson.
Used by permission.
Scripture quotations marked 'MSG' are from THE MESSAGE, copyright ©
1993, 2002, 2018 by Eugene H. Peterson. Used by permission of NavPress.
All rights reserved. Represented by Tyndale House Publishers, Inc.
Scripture quotations marked 'NIV' are from the Holy Bible, New International
Version® Anglicized, NIV® Copyright © 1979, 1984, 2011 by Biblica, Inc.®
Used by permission. All rights reserved worldwide.
Scripture quotations marked 'NLT' are from the Holy Bible, New Living
Translation, copyright © 1996, 2004, 2015 by Tyndale House Foundation.
Used by permission of Tyndale House Publishers, Inc., Carol Stream, Illinois
60188. All rights reserved.
Scripture quotations marked 'TPT' are from The Passion Translation®.
Copyright © 2017, 2018, 2020 by Passion & Fire Ministries, Inc. Used by
permission. All rights reserved. ThePassionTranslation.com.

First edition 2024
A catalogue record for this book is available from the British Library
Produced on paper from sustainable sources
Printed and bound in the UK by Clays Limited

Hello,

It's so good to meet you. OK, so we aren't actually meeting, but I feel like I know you because I've thought about you so much while writing this book.

A few things you need to know about me . . . I love cheese (cheddar, in particular) and Jesus (weirdly, that rhymes with cheeses!), and I'm a little on the bonkers side. You'll get used to it . . . I hope!

This book is filled with stories from my life - some of the most fun bits and a few moments that I found challenging.

I hope the pages of this book encourage you to spend time with your heavenly Father, to get lost in his crazy LOVE for you and to build a friendship with him so strong that nothing can shake it . . . no matter **what's up**!

Enjoy!

Love,

Joanna x

What's in the book?

1

Pick me, pick me!

I don't know about you, but I can get **sooooo easily distracted**. There are times when I walk into a room, get side-tracked, and forget what I went in for. If you've never experienced this, grab the nearest grown-up. They'll know exactly what I mean!

I'm going to tell you something. You might think this is totally bonkers . . . buuuuut, here goes . . .

When I was growing up, I only had three TV channels! Yip, you heard me . . . three!

But when I turn the TV on today there are a billion channels with programmes on 24/7. You can stream, watch on demand, and even pause the TV to go to the toilet! There are so many distractions and demands on our time and attention.

I often ask myself: what am I giving <u>my</u> attention to?

Believe it or not, we actually have a choice about what we give our time and attention to. It would be so easy to spend all weekend watching cute animal videos online, wouldn't it?

But whatever you **choose** to focus on will have an effect on you.

Where your focus goes, your energy flows!

The Bible asks us to **seek God first**.

I've been challenged over and over again to keep turning my attention to God. The truth is, he is ready and waiting for us. **He wants to spend time with us, and he wants us to spend time with him.** Sometimes I need to **choose** to turn off the TV and put down my phone so I can spend time with my heavenly Father.

DEAR GoD,

It's so easy to get distracted with all that's going on around us, but I want to choose to put you first. Help me to stay focused on you and bring you into every part of my life. In Jesus' name. Amen

What's Up WOW

There are approximately two million cat videos on YouTube, and each video has an average of 12,000 views. That's a lot of time spent watching cats, guys!

"But **seek first** his kingdom and his righteousness, and all these things will be given to you as well."

Matthew 6:33 (NIV)

How do you like to
spend your time?

 READING
 HOMEWORK
GAMING

 SPORTS
WATCHING TV
BUILDING LEGO

What's Up challenge

Set aside some time to spend with God this week.
This may involve reading a story from the Bible,
listening to worship music, or simply telling God
about your day and asking him to be with you.

How about setting a What's Up alarm
to remind you to spend time in the
presence of God each day?

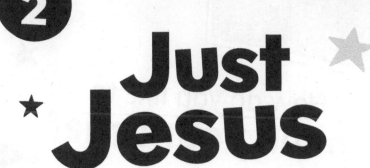

2

Just Jesus

Is there a famous person you really look up to? Maybe a football player, singer, speedcuber, or influencer?

■ YES ■ NO

The famous person I look up to is:

Is there a celebrity you love so much that you know literally everything about them - their birthday, where they grew up, all the world records they've broken, and even the kind of bubble bath they like to use? You know so much about them, yet you've never actually met them.

When I was younger, it was like that for me with Jesus.
I went to church, knew loads of Bible stories, and had
learned all about Jesus, but I didn't **really** know him.
I lived my life, having fun and making my own choices,
but Jesus wasn't really involved!

It wasn't until years later, when a friend reminded me
that God knew me personally and

I could have my own friendship with Jesus,

that I really got to know him.

I began to spend time quietly with Jesus, and asked
him to be with me as I made decisions about my life.
I could tell him everything that was going on right
there and then, and I could trust him with my future.

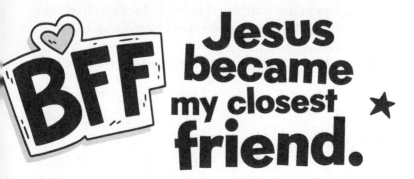

And I've never looked back!

"For God loved the world so much that **he gave his only Son.**
God gave his Son so that whoever believes in him may not be lost, but have eternal life."

John 3:16 (ICB)

When Adam and Eve ate fruit from the tree of knowledge in the garden of Eden (after God had told them not to), they were separated from God. But the good news is, God had a plan so that Adam and Eve - **and we** - could be close to him again. He sent his Son, Jesus!

Your heavenly Father created you, knows you inside out, and wants to have a close friendship with you. The best news is that this friendship can keep growing and growing!

If you want to have Jesus in your life as a friend, you can pray this simple prayer:

DEAR GOD,

Thank you for sending us your son so we could have a personal relationship with you. I don't just want to know *about* you, I want to *know* you and be close to you. Please come and be in every part of my life. In Jesus' name. Amen

A friendly choice

What's Up WOW

Did you know that whales make friends? Yip, it's true. Beluga whales make friends with other whales outside their families, just like we do. I bet they have a splashing good time!

I remember my first ever friend. She had beautiful strawberry-blonde hair, was the fastest runner in the class, and always ate a Marmite sandwich for lunch! She was awesome. We were very different, but somehow, even at four years old, I felt totally loved and accepted by her.

I remember another "friendship" I had in primary school. Let's call this friend Fiona Deen (not her real name). We were in the same class at school and her family lived near mine, but being around Fiona made me want to walk backwards into a brick wall until it swallowed me up and I disappeared. She was the kind of **unkind** that is hard to put into words.

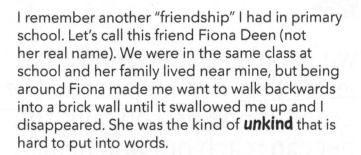

Even though I dreaded being around Fiona for fear of what she might say or do, for some very strange reason I wanted to be friends with her. I wanted her to like me.

When I left school and eventually had a friendship with Jesus for myself, I remember praying for friends. **Great** friends. And God answered my prayer BIG TIME! Now I'm overwhelmed (in a good way) with incredible friends. I have friends who encourage me and build me up so much that it literally makes me cry . . . happy tears, of course!

But throughout the ups and downs of friendships I've learned some valuable lessons:

❶ We were created for friendships.
God never intended for us to be alone.

❷ We have a choice about who we call our friends.
Great friends will encourage you to be everything that God created you to be. So choose wisely!

"Two people are better off than one, for they can help each other succeed. If one person falls, the other can reach out and help. But someone who falls alone is in real trouble."

Ecclesiastes 4:9-10 (NLT)

A **<u>GREAT</u>** friend

encourages you

doesn't compare or compete with you

laughs and cries with you

listens to you

lovingly corrects you

builds you up

makes time for you.

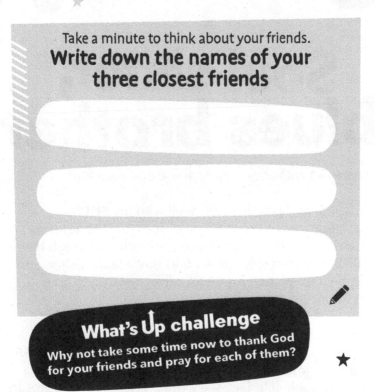

Take a minute to think about your friends.
Write down the names of your three closest friends

What's Up challenge
Why not take some time now to thank God for your friends and pray for each of them?

If the friends you have aren't **great** friends, ask God to give you the boldness to step away from those friendships, and pray for **great** friends to come into your life.

FATHER GOD,

Thank you for my friends. Help me to make good choices when choosing new friends, and help me to be a good friend to others, too. In Jesus' name. Amen

4

Soul sister, blues brother

Having a brother or sister can be so much fun!

Growing up, I got on really well with my **sister**. Our bedrooms were right next door, and at night we would spend hours talking to each other through the wall. We shared silly stories and made each other laugh so much that my sister often needed to take her inhaler!

We would also team up and play tricks on family members, build epic forts, and be each other's dinner table wingmen - helping each other to dodge eating our vegetables! In fact, we were so close that we would tell each other we were **sisters by chance, but friends by choice**.

I did, however, go through a phase of being the **annoying little sister** ... and if you know anything about me, you'll know that I was fully committed to this role! I tried to muscle in on my big sister's play dates, copied everything she said, and even borrowed her clothes - without asking!

You might have a little sister who's a tad annoying or a brother who drives you bonkers.

It can be hard when you have to share a house with someone else. Maybe you even share a bedroom and all your belongings. It's pretty normal to feel frustrated now and again, but here's the thing. God asks us to **LOVE** one another – even our annoying siblings. In fact, he especially wants us to love our annoying siblings!

It's easy to love those who show us love, and to be kind to those who are kind to us, **but God asks us to LOVE people even when that's not the case**.

God asks us to love others the way he loves us, without holding back or expecting anything in return . . . even when they are a little annoying. When we fully receive God's love in our hearts, we can start to love others this way, too.

"We love because God first loved us."

1 John 4:19 (NIV)

"And God gave us this command: Whoever loves God must also love his brother."

1 John 4:21 (ICB)

or sister!

What's Up WOW

Many years ago, a lady in Russia gave birth to a whopping sixty-nine children! She had sixteen sets of twins, seven sets of triplets, and four sets of quadruplets. Imagine having sixty-eight brothers and sisters! Now that's a whole lot of love to go around.

Circles of love

Use these circles to write something you love about your siblings. If you don't have siblings, write about your friends!

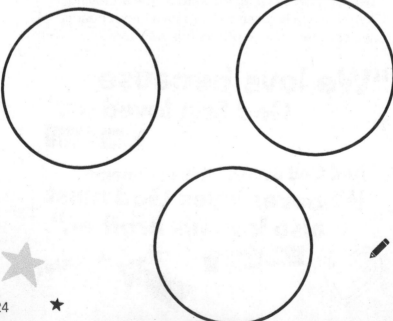

Why don't you write your own prayer?

Start by telling God how awesome he is.

WOAH _____

He's _____

Awesome

Now thank God for something that is happening in your life.

THANK YOU _____

_____

And say sorry for anything you've done that you shouldn't have.

SORRY _____

_____

U can ask God anything, just don't forget to say...

PLEASE! _____

_____

What's Up challenge

If you have a brother or sister, what can you do to show love to them this week? Could you ...

- ... offer to make them a drink?

- ... play a board game together?

- ... find some sticky notes and write a kind message for them? You could explain why you love them or say something to encourage them.

5

What goes in must come out

What's Up WOW

Apparently, if you eat a lot of beetroot you will have purply red poo and pink wee!

What goes in must come out!
It's basic science, right?
We see it everywhere . . .

If we drink loads and loads of water, eventually it'll have to **come out**, and we'll find ourselves with our legs crossed, shouting, "I need a wee, I need a weeeeeee!"

If we watch a scary movie, it might **come out** again in a bad dream.

If you eat a mega spicy curry, that has to **come out**, too. Probably into the loo . . . (Let's not go into too much detail there.)

Imagine squeezing an orange really hard with the skin on. Whatever is inside will come out . . . *hopefully just orange juice*!

If we fill our heads and hearts with God's truth - by reading the Bible and listening to worship songs - that's what will come out when WE are squeezed . . . even in the most challenging times.

Now that's the kind of **juice** I want coming out of me!

Super smoothie

Design your perfect smoothie. Remember: put good things in and good things will come out!

What's Up challenge

What great things can you **put into** your life this week? Why not try learning a Bible verse? You never know - it might just **come out** when you or someone else needs it this week.

This week I am going to...

_____

_____

_____

The Bible says that when we have the Holy Spirit in **our lives we will see** good fruit come out of us!

LOVE

JOY

PATIENCE

PEACE

DEAR JESUS,

Help me to be wise about the things I put into my life. I know that the things I watch, read, and listen to have an effect on me. Help me to make good choices and put healthy things into my mind, body, and soul. In Jesus' name. Amen

Snake eyes

NAME: Tracy Wood

JOB: Salvation Army children's leader

LIKES: Sausages and mash

DISLIKES: Spiders

FUN FACT: I have 6 sisters and 4 brothers

I need to tell you about the time I saw a HUMUNGOUS snake - a snake so huge it made me jump out of my skin and **scream**!

Have you ever been minding your own business, then all of a sudden something caught your eye and made you jump?

Well, that's exactly what happened to me when I was on holiday.

I was out in the countryside enjoying a beautiful walk. I don't know about you, but I love to look up and down when I'm walking, taking in all the nature around me. I had my binoculars, so things that were far away looked **up close and personal**. I was at one with nature! I was in my happy place . . . until I saw the snake!

Imagine me standing beside a little stream and looking out at the water. As I looked at the stream, I totally forgot that I was using my binoculars, and suddenly THERE IT WAS! Slithering in the water – a HUGE **snake**! It was green . . . it was yellow . . . its mouth was open . . . and it was **COMING MY WAY**!

I don't know what you would have done, but I let out a really loud scream, jumped back, and started to run away. As I screamed, I heard my friend start to laugh; not a quiet laugh, but a really loud, silly, in-your-face kinda laugh. It was then I realized I had been looking through my binoculars. When I took them away from my face and looked back at the water, I saw a **teeny-weeny** snake.

Phew! What had seemed to me to be something really big was actually quite small and ordinary.

The Bible reminds us to use our eyes to look up to God, because when things in our lives seem really BIG, God can give us strength and help us to see more clearly.

Tracy x

If you have something big going on right now that feels scary, share it with an adult you trust and ask them to pray with you. **God loves you so much, and he wants you to tell him when you need help with the big things in life.**

"**I lift up my eyes** to the mountains – where does my help come from?

My help comes from the LORD, the Maker of heaven and earth."

Psalm 121:1-2 (NIV)

DEAR JESUS,

When things in life feel big and scary, help me to lift my eyes to see you, and to know that you are with me. You give me strength and help me to understand the things I'm worried about. In Jesus' name. Amen

Are you finding some things in your life really big at the moment? What are they?

_____

_____

Is there anything you want to ask God to help you with?

_____

_____

Remember the Bible verse about looking up to God. Is there one BIG, exciting thing in your life that you want to thank God for?

_____

_____

What's Up WOW

Did you know that snakes use their tongues to smell? It's true! They do their best sniffing and smelling through their mouths. So if you see a snake flicking its tongue, it is probably trying to smell you!

Tune in

7

Have you ever been **lost** before? Maybe in a crowd of people or in a busy playground?

I once got lost in a superstore. I was about five years old, and was out shopping with my mum and sister. I was probably skipping around the shop, hiding in the clothes rails, and daydreaming about what I was going to have for my dinner. Before I knew it, I was all alone. I couldn't see my family anywhere! Where were they?

I wandered around the shop looking for them, trying not to go too far in case they were looking for me as well . . . After a few moments, I started to panic. I really couldn't find them.

I felt a nervous lump in my throat and tears starting to swell, so I took a deep breath. I knew exactly what I needed to do.

No matter how noisy the shop got, I would always be able to recognize my mum's voice. I knew her voice better than anything!

I decided to stay still and just listen out for her voice.

Despite all the noise, I found my mum when she called my name. I knew exactly where she was. I wrapped my arms around her and didn't let go until we got home. I don't think I ever played the "hide in the clothes rail" game again!

Tuning in to and recognizing God's voice is similar to listening to a parent or loved one. The more time we spend in the presence of God, getting to know him and reading the Bible, the more we'll recognize his voice when he speaks to us.

What's Up WOW

New South China Mall in China is one of the largest retail outlets in the world. It's a huge building at 6.46 million square-feet! There's an indoor and outdoor roller coaster, and even a canal with gondolas. You wouldn't want to get lost in there!

Four of the loudest sounds in the world are:

- the clicking of a sperm whale
- a rocket launch
- a plane taking off
- fireworks

But which one do you think is the loudest?

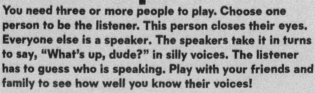

GAME

Listen up!

You need three or more people to play. Choose one person to be the listener. This person closes their eyes. Everyone else is a speaker. The speakers take it in turns to say, "What's up, dude?" in silly voices. The listener has to guess who is speaking. Play with your friends and family to see how well you know their voices!

Answer: The clicking of a sperm whale (230 dB)

"My sheep listen to my voice; I know them, and they follow me."

John 10:27 (NIV)

THANK YOU, LORD,
that I can get to know you as closely as the people I love here on earth. I want to know you and recognize your voice. Help me to stay close to you. In Jesus' name. Amen

8

You talkin' to me?

"The Lord came and stood there, calling as at the other times, 'Samuel! Samuel!'

Then Samuel said, 'Speak, for your servant is listening.'"

1 Samuel 3:10 (NIV)

When I was young, I always read this Bible story where God speaks to Samuel and thought, **WOAH!** *That's incredible!* Samuel actually *heard* God's voice. That must've been pretty crazy. If you haven't read it, you should. It's very cool.

I can't remember the first time I felt God speak to me, but it definitely wasn't in an audible voice like Samuel heard. When God speaks to me it's more like a **deep nudging in my heart**, a still, small voice or a thought being dropped into my mind.

At first it was tricky to know if it was really God, but I decided a long time ago that if I thought God was speaking to me or asking me to do something, **I'd rather do it anyway and risk getting it wrong than not do it and miss what God was saying!** Eventually, after A LOT of listening, I learned to know exactly when it was God speaking to me.

I remember sitting in church one day a few years ago and having that nudging feeling. I felt God was asking me to pray for the person next to me and to tell her not to worry because God had it covered.

Here we go, I thought. *Is she going to think I'm a complete weirdo? Maybe, but I'll do it anyway.*

So I asked if I could pray for her and shared what I felt God was saying. As I prayed, she began to cry. She told me she had recently moved away from home to study and had been really worried about how she was going to cope with all the changes in her life. After we prayed, she said she felt a sense of peace and knew that God was with her. She felt *seen* by God, and knew that he cared about her and her situation. She was encouraged . . . and so was I!

When we open our hearts to listen to God, he will most certainly speak to us.

God can speak to us in so many ways.

Perhaps in a dream or a nudging feeling in your heart. It could be a thought that jumps out at you when you read or watch something, or it could be a small idea or a picture dropped into your mind. **Be open today to any way that God wants to speak to you!**

DEAR GOD,

It's amazing that you choose to speak to us. Thank you that you care so much about what's going on in our lives. Sorry for the times when I fill my life with distractions and don't stop to listen to you. Please help me to hear your voice. In Jesus' name. Amen

What's Up challenge

Why don't you put on a worship song and spend some quiet time with God? You might want to close your eyes to help you stay focused on him. You never know - he might just drop a thought into your heart.

What do you feel God is saying?

What's Up WOW

Did you know that, when you are in a light sleep, your ears can still hear and process the sounds happening around you?

9

Blue door, red door . . . not sure

Have you ever had to make a choice, but had absolutely NO idea what to do?

I used to find it really hard to make decisions, especially if there were more than two options to choose from. (Choosing dinner at a restaurant was a nightmare!)

I remember feeling like this when I had to choose a new flat to share with some friends.

We prayed about where to live, and I felt as though the Holy Spirit was **speaking to me.** Only this time it was more like a **picture in my mind.**

In my mind I saw a **white house** with a **BLUE** door, surrounded by leaves and flowers that climbed up and around the door frame.

Eventually we made a choice and found somewhere to live. Guess what colour the door was . . . Go on . . . guess! It was . . .

RED!

A red door?! It was a tiny red door next to a fish and chip shop, which led to a flat above a dry cleaner's. There were no leaves or beautiful flowers in sight!

I was confused. What about the picture I had seen in my mind that day we prayed?

After a few weeks of living in our new flat, I looked out of my bedroom window . . . and on the other side of the road, beyond some trees, I saw a white house with a blue door, surrounded by flowers. I was absolutely gobsmacked! That was exactly the picture I had seen in my mind when we prayed.

I'll be honest with you. I **100%** thought we were going to live in that house with the blue door. But **God had a plan and a place for us**, and when I saw that house from my bedroom window, I knew I was in exactly the right place.

DEAR GOD,

Thank you that you care about every detail of our lives. The big things and the small. I know that you love me. Help me to trust you as you guide me through life, even when I don't quite know what to do. In Jesus' name. Amen

When we don't know what to do, we can pray and ask God to help us. And even if we still don't know **exactly** what to do, we know that God hears our prayers, and will be with us and guide us as we make choices!

"The LORD directs the steps of the godly. He delights in every detail of their lives."

Psalm 37:23 (NLT)

Why don't you write your own prayer?

Start by telling God how awesome he is.

WOAH
He's
Awesome

_____

_____

Now thank God for something that is happening in your life.

THANK YOU

_____

_____

And say sorry for anything you've done that you shouldn't have.

SORRY

_____

_____

U can ask God anything, just don't forget to say...

PLEASE!

_____

Spot the difference
Can you find all seven differences?

10

★
Not-so-green
★ fingers
★

What's Up WOW

Did you know that plants can communicate with each other? If an insect comes to munch on a plant's leaves, the plant produces chemicals to deter its attacker. This chemical also acts as a warning signal for other plants to let them know that insects are on the way!

One thing you should know about me is that I am the **world's worst gardener**! OK, so that's a slight exaggeration . . .

But seriously, I'm pretty bad!

My mum, on the other hand, is a wonderful gardener. She has what they call **"green fingers"** and can grow pretty much anything from a seed.

As a kid, my garden was full of strawberries, raspberries, blackberries, and gooseberries . . . every type of berry you can think of!

I decided I should take a leaf out of my mum's book (see what I did there?) and try to grow one of my fave flowers. Mum gave me a small cutting and told me how to look after it. Super gardeners like my mum can easily grow a plant from a cutting, but before the cutting can grow again it needs to regrow its roots.

I'd love to tell you that I grew my little flower and got first prize in the "redeemed gardener" category! But NO. That is not what happened. Within a few weeks, that hopeful little cutting had wilted and died. It had no roots. Even though it is possible for a plant to survive when it is cut off and uprooted, it is tricky for it to take root again.

It's the same in my relationship with God. When I start drifting away, unconsciously cutting myself off and getting distracted with "life", I can quickly become Short-tempered Shazza, Judgemental Jojo, and Worrywart Wilbur.

Just like my little cutting, **I need to stay rooted in Jesus and connected to God, my creator, in order to grow and stay healthy**. Remember that your heavenly Father wants to stay close and connected to you, too!

"I am the vine; you are the branches. If you remain in me and I in you, you will bear much fruit; apart from me you can do nothing."

John 15:4-5 (NIV)

HEAVENLY FATHER,

You love us so much, and want us to stay rooted in and connected to you. Help me to stay close to you no matter what is going on around me.
In Jesus' name. Amen

 If you unplug the TV, you won't be able to turn it on and watch it!

 If there's no internet connection, you won't be able to get online.

 If you're far away from God, you may not be able to hear his voice.

Stay connected to God, so that YOU can be all that he created you to be!

What can you do to stay connected to God?

Write down three ideas

1

2

3

What's Up challenge

Why don't you try to do one of the things on your list every day this week?

11

What if?

Worry.

It starts with a tiny seed of **what-if-shaped doubt** in your mind:

What if no one comes to my party?

What if I don't pass the exam?

What if my trainers aren't cool enough?

The **what-if** wiggles down toward your heart, anxiety sets in, and suddenly you feel sad because **you think** no one's coming to your party (even though the party hasn't even happened yet), or you feel nervous about not getting into the school you want because **you may not** pass the exam - even before you've sat it.

The emotions are real. But the circumstances aren't.

Worry continues to work its way through your body. You start to feel sick, your imagination runs wild, and you let those **what-ifs** become full-blown Netflix movies in your head!

Has that ever happened to you?

When I worry about things that are happening in my life, it's almost like saying I don't fully trust God. It's when **I try to take control** of my life that the scary and uncertain feelings set in.

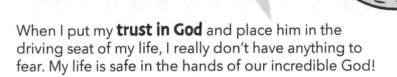

If you're feeling afraid or upset about something that's happening in your life, find a grown-up you trust to share it with. It could be a parent, a teacher or someone at church. It's not wrong to be afraid – and sometimes talking to someone about what's going on can really help.

When I put my **trust in God** and place him in the driving seat of my life, I really don't have anything to fear. My life is safe in the hands of our incredible God!

"Don't worry about anything; instead, pray about everything. Tell God what you need, and thank him for all he has done. Then you will experience God's peace, which exceeds anything we can understand. His peace will guard your hearts and minds as you live in Christ Jesus."

Philippians 4:6-7 (NLT)

Can you find these words from today's verse in the word search?

Don't worry **pray** Hearts Peace

Everything **Thankful**

Experience **Guard** Jesus

I R B M D E G A U G T N R H
G U N C Y Z I U N P H I L E
F D G G E Q D R A F A W B A
D E O X C X Y G Q T N T U R
J Y V N K Q P P A R K J A T
E A M E T S F E P W F S Z S
S X G P R W P V R D U O N T
U Y U P F Y O G A I L W B C
S T A E Q L T R Y A E G E R
E R R S P Y D H R L M N H X
C O D N Q E D Z I Y H L C R
E U A N D J A W N N M O Y E
X S X F D V U C S G G M G P
Z A N E J J G Y E Z B L P U

Why don't you take a moment to tell God anything you are worried about and ask him to be with you?

_____

_____

_____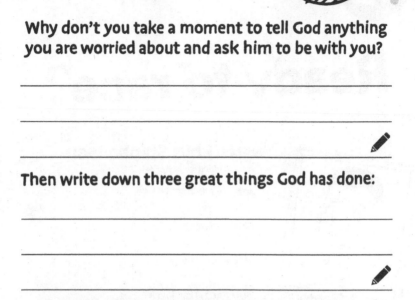

Then write down three great things God has done:

_____

_____

_____

What's Up challenge

Share what you've written with a grown-up and pray about it together.

Spend a few minutes reading your list, fixing your heart and mind on the great things God has done in your life, for those around you, or in the wider world. Thank him for these things.

DEAR JESUS,

Help me to remember that I can give you all my worries because you care for me. Help me to fix my eyes on you and to remember all the amazing things you have done. I know you are a faithful God. Replace my worries with your incredible peace. In Jesus' name. Amen

12

Ready to race?

NAME: Rhys Stephenson
Nickname: Rhysy Pips

JOB: TV presenter on CBBC

LIKES: Lasagne

DISLIKES: Porridge

FUN FACT: I can juggle!

(Strictly Come Dancing Semi-finalist)

FACT FILE

"Can we pray?" in one of the most terrifying things you can say to a non-Christian.

In Year 6, I was at the annual athletics competition between the schools in our area. My three teammates and I were getting ready to take part in the 4 x 100m relay race. As we sat on the grass waiting to be called, **I felt a sudden urge to do the one thing I only ever felt comfortable doing alone: PRAY**. But this time I knew that doing it alone wouldn't work. Somehow, even at eleven years old, I felt that if I was going to pray for my team's victory I had to include the whole team.

But ask three other kids to pray with me? What would they THINK?

Nonetheless, I took a breath and, feeling completely vulnerable, gently asked, **"Guys, can we pray?"** They turned to me, looking slightly confused, but luckily one of them smiled and nodded, then the rest followed. I couldn't believe it! I could've cried. We threw our hands into the middle, and I led the prayer.

As we said "Amen" we were called to race. The gun fired and we were off!

I was the last person in our team to run and, by the time I started running, my competitor was already ahead of me! I sprinted toward him as if I was being chased by lions – tears, sweat, and snot streaming across my face. Before I knew it I'd caught up. We were neck and neck! All I needed to do to finish first was stretch my neck out as far as I could as I crossed the finish line.

When the race was over, hundreds of people stood staring at the umpire, waiting for him to make his decision. **We had won!**

And for the first time ever I had shared my faith with other people. I had brought them into my relationship with God; that was my real victory.

Sometimes it can feel scary to talk about God, but part of the Christian journey is being brave enough to include God in every aspect of our lives because he cares about every detail.

So the next time you see an opportunity to receive God's help, call on him – even if it means doing it with others. Pray an honest prayer (not a fancy one) and see him at work in you and in those around you!

Prayer is the best way for us to communicate with God. It's how we confide in him, celebrate with him, and ask things of him. When we gather together in Jesus' name, we are often surprised at the amazing things that happen.

FATHER GOD,

Thank you that you want to be included in every part of my life because you care about me. Help me to be more open about my relationship with you, and to use the gifts you have given me to bless those around me. In Jesus' name. Amen.

What's Up WOW

Did you know that the oldest person to have run a marathon is Fauja Singh? Fauja didn't walk until he was five, but he certainly made up for that - running his last marathon in Toronto aged 100! Meanwhile, the fastest-ever recorded running speed is a whopping 27.78 mph, achieved by Jamaican sprinter Usain Bolt at the 2009 World Championships in Berlin.

GAME

Every-room relay

Choose an unbreakable item (like a teddy or a cushion) to be your baton. Ask each member of your team (family or friends) to start in a different room in your home.
Run from room to room passing the baton. The relay ends when the baton is back in the room where it started.

For example,

Player one starts in the kitchen and runs to the bedroom.

Player two runs from the bedroom to the bathroom.

Player three runs from the bathroom to the living room.

Player four runs from the living room to the kitchen.

Why not time yourselves, then see if you can break your every-room record!

My family's every-room relay record is...

What's Up challenge

Choose a friend to pray for this week. Pray for them a little each day. You could leave a sticky note with their name on by your mirror to remind you to pray for them!

This week I will pray for...

13

I am . . . ME!

I grew up in a little village in Hampshire. This village was so small that it wasn't even on the map! There was a sweet shop, a post office, a church, a fishing shop, and a rundown pub. You could literally drive from one end of the village to the other in ninety seconds.

Village life meant that pretty much everyone knew each other, and the school was no different. Within a week of starting school, we knew everyone's middle names, pets' names, pets' middle names, and even what cereal someone's grandad liked to eat on Fridays!

Even though I knew almost everyone, **I just didn't feel like I fitted in**.

The boys were great to play with, buuuuut they were boys, and I wasn't one . . .

After school I hung out with "the cool girls" (FYI, I was not cool). These girls had the coolest clothes, and they were allowed to stay out really late and watch movies I wasn't allowed to watch.

And then there were the super-clever kids. I sat with them during lessons, but I didn't really fit in there either!

I felt lost. Who was I and where did I belong?

I was so busy trying to fit in with all the others that I forgot to look to God – the one who created me – for the answers.

The truth is, God created us in HIS image, **but designed US uniquely.** There's no one else quite like you. Or me!

I didn't need to fit in with a particular group – that's not what God had designed. **He just needed me to be me.**

"I praise you because you made me in an amazing and wonderful way. What you have done is wonderful. I know this very well."

Psalm 139:14 (ICB)

Why don't you take time to thank God for the wonderful way he has made you?

DEAR GOD,

Thank you for making me so unique and wonderful. Help me to remember that I don't need to change myself to fit in with other people. You love me just the way I am. In Jesus' name. Amen

What's Up WOW

Did you know that in the same way that everyone has a unique fingerprint, we also have a unique smell?! Even identical twins smell different.

What God says about you:

free
LOVED
worthy
chosen
BLESSED
COURAGEOUS
valuable
MASTERPIECE

✏️ **Decorate this page!**

14

Oh my words!

Have you ever noticed that it's much easier to remember a harsh word than a compliment?
Insults somehow have a gravity-defying ability to stick with you, like throwing wet toilet paper onto the ceiling. (BTW, don't do that. It makes a huge mess!)

During my last year of drama school, one of the teachers asked me to audition for a pantomime.

This would mean:

acting - check ✔

dancing - double check ✔✔

and singing . . . umm . . . check?! I think . . .

Singing was never really my thing. I could hold a tune, but I just didn't have a great deal of confidence (and it was about to get a whole lot worse). Before I had a chance to attend the audition, one of the directors at my school told my teacher, "She's not a singer", and not to bother sending me to the audition.

Pause for a second . . . You know that feeling of being punched in the stomach so hard it makes you feel sick and want to cry? That's how I felt.

I'd love to tell you that I got myself together, smashed the audition, landed the part, and was told my voice was better than Beyoncé's!

Sadly, that wasn't the case. **Instead, I carried these harsh words around with me for years,** believing I couldn't sing. These words about who I was affected my confidence for YEARS and YEARS.

If I could go back in time, I'd definitely choose a different response. I wouldn't allow someone else's words to shape me, or to steal my joy and confidence. In fact, I'm so stubborn now that if you tell me I can't do something, I work my butt off just to prove that I can!

But this experience taught me something . . .

Proverbs 18:21a (ICB) says: "What you say can mean life and death" and it really is true! **Our words are powerful. They can build people up or tear them down.**

We can choose.

" . . . The tongue is a small part
of the body yet it carries great power!"

James 3:5 (TPT)

63

What's Up WOW

There are an estimated 1,022,000 words in the English language, and this number increases by thousands each year. But interestingly, we only regularly use about 171,476 of them. Imagine how many words there must be in all the languages in all the world!

Why not take a moment to sit with Jesus? Think about the past few days. How have you used your words?

HEAVENLY FATHER,

I know that words are powerful. Help me to be wise with my words, using them to encourage and build others up. Sorry for the times when I have been unkind with my words. Help me to think before I speak and to always use my words for good. In Jesus' name. Amen

What's Up challenge

Why not think about how you can use your words to encourage someone this week? Write someone a note telling them how proud you are of them, or tell someone in your family why you love them.

GAME

Word play

You need two or more people to play this game.

The first person says a word (any word), then each player has to say a word linked to the word they've just heard. For example, fish, water, drink, tea, time, clock, tick, insect . . .

If you repeat a word that has already been said or there is no link between your word and the last word, you are out!

GenerouSUEty

Do you have any friends you want to be just like?

■ YES ■ NO

I've got a friend like that. Her name is Sue and she's pretty awesome. I remember her telling me she had decided to be a generous person. She wasn't just going to *try to be*, she was *going to be* generous! I thought that was really cool, so I decided to be a generous person too!

Around this time, I had another friend who told me she desperately wanted to study dance. She'd found a dance school and a course she wanted to do, but it was going to cost her a lot of money to do it. **I wanted to be generous, but I didn't know how to help her.**

A few weeks later I was at a church weekend away, which was brilliant. The time came when the leaders asked people to give generously to help fund the weekend away for other people the following year. I strapped on my Sue vibes and decided to be generous.

Fast-forward a few weeks, and I received a cheque in the mail. It was – almost to the penny – twenty-five times the amount I had given away at the church event.

I knew exactly what to do with the money. I was going to help my friend pay for her dance course!

I felt so encouraged. **I'd been generous, been blessed myself, and was then able to bless someone else. This was amazing!**

You're probably thinking, *Errr I'm still in school and I've got no money.* **How can I be generous?!** But generosity isn't just about money.

You can be generous with your time – perhaps helping out at school or at church.

You can be generous with your love, with your kindness, and with your words toward others.

Maybe you could call a relative you haven't spoken to in a while or spend time with someone in the playground who looks like they need a friend.

The amazing thing is that, when we are generous and bless others, God always blesses us too!

"The world of the generous gets larger and larger;
the world of the stingy gets smaller and smaller.
The one who blesses others is abundantly blessed;
those who help others are helped."

Proverbs 11:24-25 (MSG)

Generousi-body

Can you think of a way to be generous with different parts of your body?

What's Up challenge

Why don't you look for an opportunity to be generous this week? Start small - it doesn't need to be a grand gesture.

Here are some ideas:

- Share sweets with a sibling or friend
- Share a smile with a stranger
- Share a joke with someone to make them smile
- Offer to help get plates and cutlery ready for dinner
- Ask your kids' church leaders or teachers if you can help them
- Share a hug

Why don't you add your own ideas?

DEAR JESUS,

I know that when I'm generous it blesses those around me, but it can also bless me too! Help me to be a generous person at every opportunity. Amen

16

P. R. A. Why?

What's Up WOW

Did you know that "prayer" is mentioned approximately 650 times in the Bible (depending on the version you read)?

What do we do when our prayers aren't answered?

This is a tough question - one that I definitely don't feel I have the answer to - but I'm throwing it out there anyway.

There have been times when I've prayed and haven't seen the answers to prayer I was expecting.

At those times **I've had to CHOOSE to still trust God**. That can be hard. Like REALLY hard!

I found this especially difficult when I spent years praying for a friend to be healed from cancer, but sadly she wasn't.

We see our situations with a **temporary perspective**. But God sees things with an **eternal perspective**.

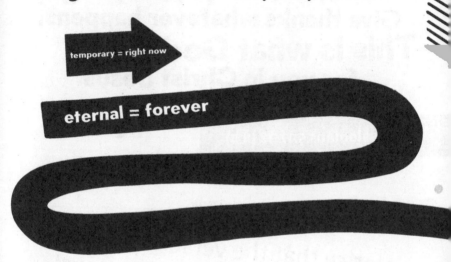

temporary = right now

eternal = forever

In the Lord's Prayer, we pray, "Your will be done." This means we have to let go of wanting things to go our own way, and trust that God's ways and thoughts are higher than ours.

The Bible tells us that in heaven there is no more sickness and no more pain. So even though my friend may not have been healed here on earth, in heaven she's completely healed and whole.

Search online for the full Lord's Prayer or look up Matthew 6:9-13 in the Bible.

"Never stop praying.
Give thanks whatever happens.
This is what God wants
for you in Christ Jesus."

1 Thessalonians 5:17-18 (ICB)

Notice that the verse tells us to give thanks **whatever happens**! Even when things don't look great, we can still give thanks.

An attitude of
gratitude

Can you write down three things you are thankful for today?

1 _____

2 _____

3 _____

What's Up challenge

Why don't you make a gratefulness jar? Every day, write something you are grateful for on a piece of paper and put it in the jar. At the end of the week, pick out some of the pieces of paper and use them to remind yourself of how awesome God is, and of the amazing things happening in your life.

HEAVENLY FATHER,

Prayer is a wonderful way to connect with you. Help us to trust you even when our prayers aren't answered in the way we expect them to be, and to remember that you love us and always want the best for us. In Jesus' name. Amen

17

Climb your tree

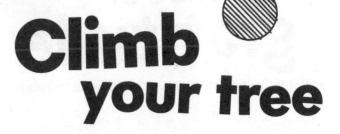

Have you ever...

... been picked **last** in sports?

... been given only **one** line in a play?

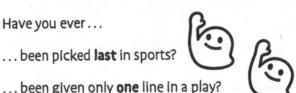

... been given a **boring** baked potato for lunch when everyone else had pizza?

Yup, yes, ya ha!

For years I felt like other people were always chosen before me. I was definitely not the most popular. In fact, I felt like the most **unpopular**!

But the truth is, we are **all** known and **chosen** by God. He loves each one of us – and we don't even need to do anything to deserve it! In the same way that our fingerprints are completely different, the opportunities and good things God has in store for us are different, too.

Imagine a garden full of trees; each one different, but perfectly designed for one person to climb it. There's one tree perfectly designed for **you**. The branches are evenly spaced and just the right size for your arms and legs to reach as you climb.

Your tree is perfect for you!

There are loads of other great-looking trees that might lead to exciting adventures ... but they weren't designed for you.

Over the years, I've learned that there is **no point comparing myself to others**. They aren't ME! Of course their lives will look different. They'll have great things happen, but so will I. And so will you! There's no point standing on the ground watching someone else climb their tree and thinking, "I wish my life looked like that," meanwhile forgetting to climb your own tree!

I want to encourage you not to compare yourself with anyone else. God delights in each one of us, and he has a perfect plan just for you.

"Surely your goodness and love will follow me all the days of my life."

Psalm 23:6 (NIV)

75

"God has chosen you and made you his holy people. He loves you. So always do these things: Show mercy to others; be kind, humble, gentle, and patient."

Colossians 3:12 (ICB)

HEAVENLY FATHER,

Thank you that you love me so much, that you chose me, and that you have a plan for my life. Help me to feel confident about the incredible things you have in store for me, and to cheer on others around me who are doing well. In Jesus' name. Amen

What's Up challenge

Next time you see one of your friends doing well, why not choose to cheer them on as they climb their tree?

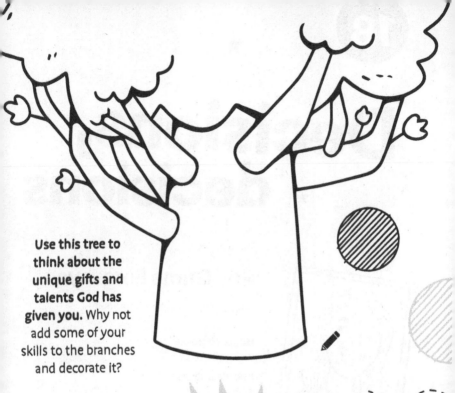

Use this tree to think about the unique gifts and talents God has given you. Why not add some of your skills to the branches and decorate it?

What's Up WOW

Did you know that goats are exceptional tree climbers? Our four-legged friends are attracted to the fruit that sits at the top of the argan tree. They are so nimble that they can reach all the way to the top of the tree. Now that's impressive!

18

Decisions, decisions

FACT FILE

NAME: Emma Borquaye

JOB: Digital strategist/author/mum

LIKES: Chocolate

DISLIKES: Cheese

FUN FACT: I like cheese on pizza!

Making decisions has never been one of my strengths. Throughout school I was asked, **"What do you want to be when you're older?"** And I never knew! Sometimes I'd say a vet, other times a TV presenter or a teacher. When it came to the end of my school years, and I had to choose if I wanted to go to university or not – and what to study if I did go – I still had no idea!

I enjoyed horse riding, so I got a place at university studying "equine management", which is looking after horses. However, two weeks before I was meant to start I completely changed my mind. I wanted to go travelling instead! I told the university I no longer needed my place, got a job at a shoe shop, and saved up to go to Australia, where I ended up having **an amazing year, full of adventure**.

There are always lots of decisions to make in life, some small and some HUGE, and sometimes we can feel afraid in our decision-making, as if our whole lives depend on one choice. This can make it even harder to choose anything for fear of getting it wrong.

But there's some really good news! The Bible says: **"We can make our plans, but the Lord determines our steps." (Proverbs 16:9, NLT)**.

This means that we are free to dream big about what we want to do with our lives, and we can trust that God will be the one who puts in place whatever is meant to be in our future. Although we may sometimes end up taking a bit of a detour, there's always an adventure to be had when we decide to do it with God.

What's Up WOW

Emma shared that she loves taking care of horses, BUT did you know that horses can't BURP?! They can't throw up or breathe through their mouths, either. A horse's digestive system is a one-way street. In one way and out the other!

How do you see God?

Seeing God as a friend rather than a strict ruler can help bring more freedom and excitement to what is in store for your life! It's not about never putting a foot wrong; instead, it's about inviting Jesus to be on the journey with you.

DEAR JESUS,

I may not know right now what my future holds, but I'd like to invite you to be on the adventure with me and help me figure it out along the way! Amen

Fantastic future

"**Be strong and courageous.
Do not be afraid or terrified
because of them, for the LORD**
your God goes with you; he will never
leave you nor forsake you."

Deuteronomy 31:6 (NIV)

Write down (or draw) any dreams or plans
you have for your future.

Robbers and roly-polies

Have you ever had a bad day? I mean a **really bad** day … that turned into a bad week? One where you felt like absolutely everything that could possibly go wrong, went wrong?

I had a week like that not so long ago…

To kick things off, I lost my glasses. This was not good because, well, I couldn't really see properly. I looked all over the house but couldn't find them anywhere. Then I got hit in the head with a wooden door and ended up at A&E. The blow caused so much pain that I had to pay an emergency visit to the dentist, who told me I needed some intense dental work. Then, to top it off, a young family member did a roly-poly over a pencil and badly jabbed himself in the leg (the pencil was fine – the leg wasn't!).

And just when I thought the storm was over, I woke up on the Saturday morning to discover that my car had been broken into. All my belongings had been thrown around the car and a pair of brand-new roller skates had been stolen from the boot. I could feel my pulse beginning to race … everything in me wanted to **scream**!

But in this moment I had a choice to make.
Was I going to get upset, be grumpy for the rest
of the weekend and walk around with a face like a
hippopotamus's bottom?

OR was I somehow going to seek God in this?

Was God in it? How could he possibly be in such a
terrible situation?

As I sat in the driver's seat of my car, it took everything
within me to make the choice not to focus on what was
happening but to **fix my eyes on God**. I told myself
that even though my circumstances had changed and
looked really bad, God doesn't change . . . and he was
still good!

I decided to look for something positive in the
situation. At least I still had a car! That was something
to be thankful for.

I looked down, and at my feet was a pair of glasses.
My glasses! The ones I'd looked for everywhere.
When the robbers ransacked the car, they found my
glasses and left them - undamaged! - in the footwell
of the driver's seat. Something else to be thankful for.

Before I even had a chance to get my grump on,
I began to feel a sense of peace. *God's* peace. Even in
the craziness of my week I could feel God with me.

I want to encourage you to hold on to God when the
storms come. Life might get a little crazy and the winds
might blow (it may even feel like a tornado!), but God is
stable. He doesn't change and he is always with us.

"We have troubles all around us, but we are not defeated. We do not know what to do, but we do not give up. We are persecuted, but God does not leave us. We are hurt sometimes, but we are not destroyed."

2 Corinthians 4:8-10 (ICB)

Would you rather have someone . . .

. . . drop worms in your cereal

— OR —

. . . accidently put spicy sauce in your hot chocolate?

Next time you're having a bad day, take a moment to **stop and find the good in it!**

DEAR LORD,

Even when life is tough, you are with me. Nothing is too much for you. No matter how bad my day might be, you are still good – and there is always something to be thankful for. In Jesus' name. Amen

What's Up challenge

Write down three things you are thankful for:

1 _____

2 _____

3 _____

20

Oops, it was me . . .

Have you ever messed up? I mean, really messed up?! Well, I have – many times. Let me tell you about one of them . . .

As a kid, my mum constantly used to tell me to stop swinging on my chair. Sound familiar? ;-) Needless to say, **I did not listen**. One day at dinner I was, as usual, swinging on my chair, and before I knew it there was an almighty CRASH!

You're probably thinking I fell off my chair.

Nope!

I fell backwards through the pane of glass that separated the dining room from the living room. There was no escaping this one! I couldn't blame my sister, I couldn't blame the rabbit, I couldn't blame ANYONE! It was one of those "Oops! It was me!" moments. It was *definitely* my fault.

Everybody in the house stopped as they realized what had happened. I started to feel awful. Not only because there was broken glass all over the floor, but because I had been doing something I'd been told **not to do** over and over again. I had *really* messed up.

I can't remember what my mum and dad said to me in that moment, but somehow, even though I'd totally messed up, I knew they still **LOVED** me. There were still consequences for me to face. I was probably banned from eating at the table and had to eat my food on the floor with the cat. (That's a joke, we didn't have a cat!) But although the glass was shattered all over the floor, our relationship wasn't. And even more amazingly, I didn't have a single scratch on me!

It's exactly like that with God, but even more so. We might make mistakes and get things wrong, but he still loves us.

Will we make mistakes and mess up again? **Definitely.**

Is God still madly in love with us? **Absolutely!**

There is nothing you can do to stop God from loving you. And I mean **NOTHING**! Isn't that incredible?

HEAVENLY FATHER,

When I get things wrong and make mistakes, help me to come to you and not hide away. I know that your love for me is bigger than any mistakes I could make. Thank you for your incredible, unshakeable love for me! In Jesus' name. Amen

"The LORD is gracious and compassionate, slow to anger and rich in love."

Psalm 145:8 (NIV)

Decorate this page! ✏️

88

What's Up WOW

The earliest chairs date back to Ancient Egyptian times. However, only kings and queens were allowed to sit on them back then. You and I would have had to sit on rocks! At least you can't swing back on a rock and fall off!

Why don't you write your own prayer?

Start by telling God how awesome he is.

WOAH
He's
Awesome
_____
_____

Now thank God for something that is happening in your life.

THANK YOU
_____

And say sorry for anything you've done that you shouldn't have.

SORRY
_____
_____

U *can ask God anything, just don't forget to say...*

PLEASE!
_____

21

Funky forgiveness

We all mess up - like the time I broke the glass after repeatedly swinging on my chair . . . or the time my sister and I decided to play "throw the cushions" in the living room and broke the glass light fittings. (Oh, I haven't told you about that, have I?) My point is this: **we all make mistakes**, some big and some small. And even though I know that - just as my parents did - God forgives me when I mess up, there have been times when I've found it hard to forgive myself.

Have you ever felt like that?

Have you ever felt guilty about something you've done, questioning if God could really still love you? The great news is, HE DOES!

The Bible says our wrongdoings are removed from us as far as the EAST is from the WEST. Now I'm not great at geography, but I do know that east and west are as far away from one another as they could possibly be!

I had to remind myself that when Jesus died on the cross and rose again, he wiped the slate clean and gave us the confidence we need to walk with our heads held high. He paid the price for our mistakes IN FULL. And because of that, when God looks at you he's not concerned with the mess; he just loves you.

So maybe you're having a hard time forgiving yourself for something that's happened. Well, let me tell you that God is more concerned with having you close to him than he is about your mess!

We can come to him, mess and all.

> When we receive his love, we can truly receive his forgiveness – and forgive ourselves, too.

"Farther than from a sunrise to a sunset – **that's how far you've** removed our guilt from us."

Psalm 103:12 (TPT)

Has something happened that you've been feeling bad about?

Imagine if Jesus were next to you right now. What do you think he'd say to you?

Use this space to write down your thoughts and prayers:

_____

_____

_____

_____

HEAVENLY FATHER,

Thank you that you are full of grace, love, and compassion. Thank you that you sent your Son, Jesus, to die on the cross and pay the price for all we've done wrong. Help me to come close to you and not to run from you when I mess up. Help me to receive your forgiveness and to forgive myself, too. In Jesus' name. Amen

Can you count the number of hearts in this picture?

REMEMBER:
NO MATTER
WHAT,
GOD
LOVES
YOU!!!!!!

22

Dirt in my face

Has anyone ever deliberately done something to hurt you?

 YES NO

When I was at primary school, there was a little boy who *really* didn't like me. One day in the playground he grabbed a pile of grit and sand from the ground and threw the dirt right into my eyes.

I remember that day like it was yesterday. I cried so much that my teachers had no choice but to call my mum and ask her to come to the school to calm me down.

The grit and dirt stung my eyes, and the whole experience deeply hurt my feelings. But through it I learned a few things about forgiveness . . .

❶ Forgiveness is totally weird!

I mean, who has their toe stamped on and says, "Oh, that's cool. I forgive you"? No one! Most of the time our natural response is to stamp right back on the other person's toe! But God asks us to be different; to forgive others the way he forgives us.

That doesn't mean we should ignore it when someone hurts us and say "That's OK." It's not OK! It wasn't OK for me to have dirt thrown in my face, and it's not OK for people to hurt each other. We should speak out when things aren't right – and there are often consequences to face.

❷ Forgiveness is freedom!

Unforgiveness hurts us more than it hurts the other person or people!

The little boy who threw dirt at me would have been told off and maybe missed his playtime, but after a few days he had probably completely forgotten about what he did. But I carried around the sadness of what had happened for weeks, and that sadness easily turned into anger and bitterness.

Anger and bitterness are like a **poison** inside us. It's not good for anyone!

When I was finally able to forgive that boy, I felt **free**! Even though what he'd done was wrong, I realized I didn't have to carry that anger around any more!

What's Up WOW

Apparently, some studies have shown that forgiveness can have huge benefits for our health, helping us sleep, reducing our blood pressure, and even decreasing our stress levels!

"Therefore, as God's chosen people, holy and dearly loved, clothe yourselves with **compassion, kindness, humility, gentleness and patience.** Bear with each other and forgive **one another** if any of you has a grievance **against someone.** Forgive as the Lord forgave you."

Colossians 3:12 (NIV)

HEAVENLY FATHER,

Sometimes people hurt our feelings. Even though it's hard, please give me the strength to forgive others the way you forgave me. In Jesus' name. Amen

Is there someone you'd like to forgive?

Why not take a moment to sit quietly with Jesus and ask him to help you forgive that person? You might want to close your eyes to help you stay focused.

Imagine putting the "thing" that person did to hurt you into a box and handing it over to God.

 Make sure you talk to a grown-up you trust about what has happened!

What's Up challenge

Ask God to help you to see the person who hurt you with different eyes. To see them as a son or daughter of God, just like you and me; as someone who is loved just like us and who messes up just like we do!

Level up!

If you feel like you've been able to forgive someone today, how about saying a positive prayer for that person? That might feel really hard! If you're not at that point yet, keep asking God for help.

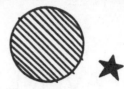

Spoons

Have you ever felt so angry that you wanted to throw something right across the room?

Has there ever been something that's made you soooo mad that you felt your body getting **HOT**, and all you wanted to do was let out an enormous **SCREAM**?

I have!

Everyone gets frustrated, and even angry, from time to time. It's pretty normal.

When I was younger, my sister and I made up a game called "Spoons". We used to bounce spoons into a metal sink and watch them fly back out. *Ping, ping, ping!* Spoons started as a game, but later became an outlet at times when we felt frustrated.

It's not wrong to feel anger; it's what we do with that anger that matters.

Sometimes we get angry when we see someone being treated unfairly, and use that frustration and passion to help change things to make their situation better!

God asks us not to sin in our anger. So screaming, shouting, and punching someone in the face are all bad ideas! We have to find healthy ways to deal with our frustration.

> Taking some time away from the thing that's making you feel angry is always a good idea.

Remember that you can be 100% real with God. When you start to feel angry, tell him all about it and allow God to give you his peace so you can deal with whatever's happening without losing your cool.

What's Up WOW

Did you know that there are more than fifty varieties of spoon? They range from caviar spoons and mustard spoons to iced tea spoons and fruit spoons. Apparently, there is a man in Australia who owns more than 30,000 teaspoons. He must have a huge cutlery drawer . . . or maybe he just really likes playing the Spoons game!

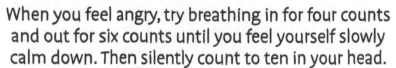

When you feel angry, try breathing in for four counts and out for six counts until you feel yourself slowly calm down. Then silently count to ten in your head.

1, 2, 3, 4 . . .

1, 2, 3, 4, 5, 6 . . .

1, 2, 3, 4, 5, 6, 7, 8, 9, 10 . . .

"When you are angry, do not sin. And do not go on being angry all day."

Ephesians 4:26 (ICB)

DEAR JESUS,

Sometimes I feel angry and frustrated. I know it's normal to feel this way now and then. Sorry for the times when I've lost my temper. Help me to take the time I need to calm down so I can talk through what's upsetting me. In Jesus' name. Amen

SUPER SPOON

★

Decorate me!

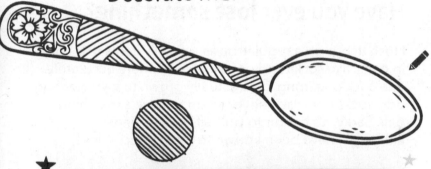

What's Up challenge

Next time you feel frustrated, why not try stepping away from the situation and telling God about it? You could write it down, draw it, or even put some music on and dance it out!

Use this space to write down how you are feeling:

★

24

Good grief

Have you ever **lost something**?

I lose things on a regular basis – usually items that come in pairs, like socks and earrings . . . or, more accurately, one sock or earring. (I've actually grown to love wearing odd socks because I never seem to have a matching pair. Sadly, it's harder to pull off odd earrings . . . although I have been known to do it on occasion!)

I always feel a bit sad when I lose one of my earrings. First, I get annoyed with myself for not taking better care of my belongings, and then there's this sense of sadness and separation when I realize I'm never going to see it again.

When a friend or family member passes away, it's like those feelings of sadness and separation are magnified by a billion. It can stir up all kinds of emotion – from feeling angry to wondering if we could have done anything to change things; from asking why this has happened to feelings of deep sadness and confusion. Sometimes we can hardly believe it's real.

This happened to me when I lost a friend at school. I was fourteen years old and everybody in the class was out on work experience. I'd gone to work at my dance school and my friend Katie had a placement at the local supermarket. During those two weeks away from school, Katie had an asthma attack. She was taken to hospital, but sadly never came home. For months after the funeral service, I sat in the classroom thinking that Katie would walk through the door and tell us it was all a mistake. I just couldn't believe it was real.

You may have experienced a loss like this, or you may have felt loss in a different way. Perhaps you felt the loss of a friendship when a good friend transferred to a new school, the loss of a pet, or the loss of your family as you knew it when your parents separated.

We all cope with loss differently, but it's important to go through the natural process of grief and healing.

It's a lot to deal with by yourself, so be sure to talk to the people around you about how you're feeling. God is incredible and can use the people around us to comfort us in times of need; to be a listening ear, to give us a hug, or to share an encouraging thought.

And of course you can talk to God too!

"The LORD is close to all whose hearts are crushed in pain, and he is always ready to restore the repentant one."

Psalm 34:18 (TPT)

Jesus said to his disciples before he went to be with his Father in heaven . . . "Now you are sad. But I will see you again and you will be happy. And no one will take away your joy."

John 16:22 (ICB)

HEAVENLY FATHER,

Losing a loved one is probably one of the hardest things we can go through. Stay close to us, Lord. Bring great people to comfort and encourage me when I feel sad. In Jesus' name. Amen

Memory box

If you've lost someone perhaps you could create a memory box. Add special memories of times spent with that person and write down all the things you loved about them!

25

Mould vs me

As a kid, I was the spider rescuer of the house when my dad was away for work. I was never afraid of spiders, so I was the one my mum and sister would call on whenever one of our eight-legged friends crawled into the house. While they stood on chairs and **screamed**, I showed the spider out!

My spider-rescuing duties were going well, until one day I walked into the bathroom and was faced with **THE BEAST**! It was the most jaw-droppingly humungous spider I'd ever seen! I literally froze with fear. What was this oversized, hairy arachnid doing in **MY** bathroom? How did it even get in there? It was huge!

For a long time I felt that same fear about **mould**. It's weird, I know, but growing up I did not like anything that was mouldy! Mould on food was the worst! I would totally freak out if I saw it. In fact, I'd rather have a big hairy spider in my bathroom than let mouldy food come anywhere near me!

But here's what I've learned about fear:

① Fear can be put into perspective

The truth is, I was a million times bigger than that spider.
It was not going to pounce on me and wrestle me to
my bathroom floor! At that moment my brain told me
I had something to fear. But when I put the spider into
perspective, I realized I had nothing to worry about.

② God is with me, whatever I face

In 1 John 4:4 (NLT), we read: **"The Spirit who lives in
you is greater than the spirit who lives in the world."**

Does that mean we'll never feel fear? Of course not!

Do huge hairy spiders and mouldy food still freak me
out? Absolutely!

But with God's Spirit in me I can face my fears.

What's Up WOW

The Goliath birdeater is the largest
spider in the world. In fact, it's
so big that it could probably sit
comfortably on your toilet!

"So do not fear, for I am with you; do not be dismayed for I am your God."

Isaiah 41:10a (NIV)

 Decorate the page.

Courage is not about having NO FEAR; it's about moving forward and doing the things that scare you anyway! Don't let **fearful feelings** stop you.

What's Up challenge

Why not spend some quiet time with God? Tell him about the things you find scary. Ask him to be with you, and allow him to fill you with his peace today.

FACING MY FEARS

FATHER GOD,

Thank you that you are always with me. Sometimes I'm afraid of...

But I know that you are bigger than anything I fear. Help me to have courage, and to know that with your Holy Spirit inside me I can face anything. In Jesus' name. Amen

26

Go, Braves, go!

"If God is for us, who can be against us?"

Romans 8:31b (NIV)

About ten years ago I went on holiday to Atlanta. My uncle worked at a baseball stadium and got us tickets to see the Atlanta Braves play. It was AWESOME!

I'd never watched a live sports game before, but I fully got into it! I had the giant hand and the giant hotdog, and every time someone hit the ball I jumped out my seat and screamed, "RUUUUUUUUUUUUUN!"

I didn't know any of the players' names and, being British, I only just about understood the rules. But I was totally invested in the players. I wanted them to succeed.

It made me think, "That's how God feels about us – but a BILLION times more! Every time we take a step forward, he's like, 'Come on! You can do it!'"

It says in the Bible that **God is for you**. That means he wants you to succeed - just like I wanted those baseball players to succeed, but even more!

It goes even further and says that **if he is for us, WHO can be against us?!**

I can only imagine how it felt for those baseball players, with tens of thousands of people cheering them on. Picture the God of the universe standing on the sidelines of your life - full of love and cheering you on!

Now that's a confidence booster!

YOU ARE LOVED

I AM FOR YOU

THERE'S NOTHING THAT CAN SEPARATE YOU FROM MY LOVE

I ADORE YOU

MY GRACE IS SUFFICIENT FOR YOU

Consider sticking some notes up around your bedroom to remind yourself how God feels about you.

Why don't you write your own prayer?

Start by telling God how awesome he is.

WOAH
He's
Awesome

_____
_____
_____

Now thank God for something that is happening in your life.

THANK YOU

_____
_____

And say sorry for anything you've done that you shouldn't have.

SORRY

_____
_____

U *can ask God anything, just don't forget to say...*

PLEASE!   _____

Double
What's Up challenge

1 Can you think of some ways to cheer on your friends and family this week?

2 Sometimes it's important to encourage yourself, too. Can you make up a chant? Imagine what God might say about you if he was cheering you on.

27

Handling pride

NAME: Pete Sheath
(which if you say it fast enough can sound like 'Peachy')

JOB: Creative Director at Studio 44 Media

LIKES: FRUIT!!!

DISLIKES: Spicy Food

FUN FACT: I grew up on the Isle of Man

FACT FILE

When I was about ten years old, my brothers and I used a rope to construct a zip wire in our back garden called the **Death Slide**. It wasn't very long, but it was steep, and it travelled downhill from one tree to another.

We used an old pair of handlebars to get down the rope, and we did this so often that we became really good at it.

THE END

Yeah, OK, that's not the end. But the next bit is embarrassing! Oh, OK, then. I'll continue . . .

One day my younger brother's friend came to play. We showed him the zip wire and explained that the best way to enjoy it was to hold on tight and not go too fast. He loved it!

Everything was going smoothly until his older sister, Sadie, came to pick him up.

Now, I have to confess that I fancied his older sister and, in a **pride-fuelled moment**, I decided to show her just how good I was at the DEATH SLIDE.

I strode over to the tree comfortably, climbed it with the greatest of ease, and then shot headfirst down the wire at top speed.

When I woke up in hospital, I saw my parents standing over me with worried expressions on their faces, concerned that I'd done something rather foolish.

They were right!

Because I was carrying so much speed, my hands had let go of the handlebars and I swung off at high speed. I winded myself and my back was badly sprained. By showing off, I had not only ruined my chances with Sadie, but my poor little brother's play date had also come to an abrupt end.

Thank goodness we don't ever have to pretend we're something we're not with God! He loves us because he loves us, and that will never change. You don't have to show off to impress him or to prove that you can handle the Death Slide. And if you truly believe that, I have a feeling it will help you with every other relationship in your life.

The Bible is FULL of promises God has given to us.
Here are a few of them for you:

Don't be afraid, he is with you.

You are a new creation.

God knew you before you were born.

You are his child.

You are royalty.

 Decorate the page.

What's Up challenge

Why don't you try turning these promises on p. 116 into "I" statements and saying them to yourself every day this week?

I don't need to be afraid, because God is with me!

I am a new creation.

_____

_____

_____

_____

DEAR GOD,

Thank you that I am treasure in your eyes. I don't have to be the best at something for you to love me. Help me to remember that you delight in me, and that's all that matters. Fill my heart with your love, and may everything in my life flow from it. In Jesus' name. Amen

Anger's BFF

As I got older, I realized something about anger. If you look closely enough, it usually has a **BFF** . . .

. . . and for me this BFF was **hurt**. Hurt from being rejected and having my trust broken, which got wrapped up in fear like a burrito. When poked, that fear of rejection and broken trust leaked out in an explosion of anger, just like hot sauce falling out of a tightly packed tortilla wrap.

I actually didn't want to be angry. I knew that this kind of anger was unhealthy and not at all productive. But believe it or not, it took me years to realize that instead of trying to deal with my anger, **I needed God to deal with the cause of that anger**: the deep hurt; the fear of being rejected and having my trust broken.

I asked God to replace these feelings of rejection with his acceptance, and to fill me with his overwhelming love. After all, **perfect love drives out all fear**.

Things didn't change in an instant, but the more I kept being filled with his love and acceptance, the less angry I became.

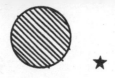

So I want to encourage you. If you find yourself feeling angry a lot (like I did), ask the Holy Spirit to show you why. What is *your* anger's BFF?

Give it to God and ask him to help you.

It may not happen overnight, and you might need to keep asking him for help, but God is faithful. He will meet you exactly where you are and give you EVERYTHING you need.

"My dear brothers and sisters, take note of this: everyone should be quick to listen, slow to speak and slow to become angry."

James 1:19 (NIV)

119

The breathing star

Use your finger to follow the sides of the star.
Breathe in and out slowly as you go around.

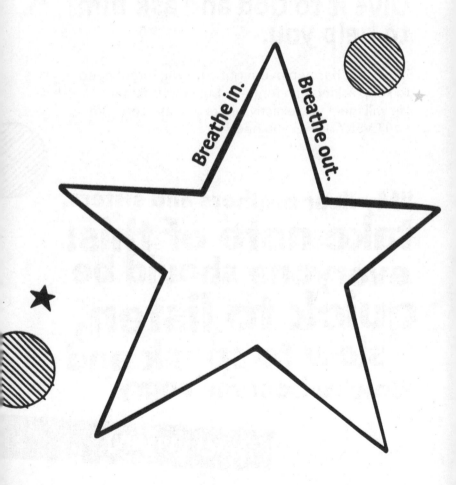

What's Up challenge

Why don't you spend some time talking to God about anything that makes you feel angry?

A prayer for when you feel angry

HEAVENLY FATHER,

I feel angry when...

I feel hurt when...

Help to heal my hurt and free me from my feelings of anger. Fill me with your incredible peace. In Jesus' name. Amen

29

Massive machete

When I was about nine years old, we went to visit one of my dad's cousins, who had moved to England from Jamaica. Within minutes of arriving at his house, he had pulled out a raw coconut . . . and a massive machete!

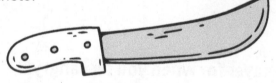

I tried to keep a polite smile on my face, but my eyes almost popped out of my head!

I had never seen a knife bigger than my mum's vegetable knife.

What on earth was that? The blade was as long as my arm – probably longer – and it looked like something from a ninja superhero movie!

This was not the time to make a fuss about disliking coconut.

In a single swipe, the machete cut the coconut in half.

The word of God (that's the Bible) is described as a double-edged sword. Sharp and powerful, it can cut through anything – just like the machete.

But how do we use the word of God like a sword?

I have often used it to cut through negative thoughts.

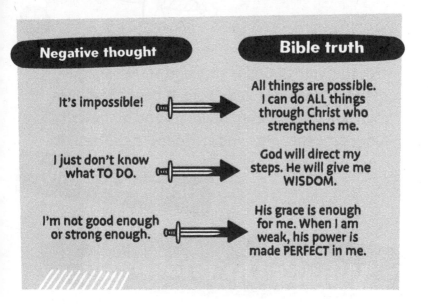

Negative thought		Bible truth
It's impossible!	→	All things are possible. I can do ALL things through Christ who strengthens me.
I just don't know what TO DO.	→	God will direct my steps. He will give me WISDOM.
I'm not good enough or strong enough.	→	His grace is enough for me. When I am weak, his power is made PERFECT in me.

The **word of God is the truth** and can cut through anything.

Keep the sword of God's word in your heart so you can pull it out and use it to help you whenever you need it!

What's Up WOW

In the mythical story about the Sword in the Stone, the sword Excalibur could only be removed from the stone, and then used, by one special person: King Arthur. But did you know that the word of God (that's the Bible!), or the sword of the Spirit, can be used by absolutely everyone? We are royalty in the kingdom of God!

"For the word of God is alive and active. Sharper than any double-edged sword, it penetrates even to dividing soul and spirit, joints and marrow; it judges the thoughts and attitudes of the heart."

Hebrews 4:12 (NIV)

What's Up challenge

Choose an encouraging Bible verse to learn this week. (There are more at the back of this book to choose from.) Write it on a sticky note and stick it on your bedroom wall. You can add more in the days and weeks to come.

Code breaker Can you crack the code?

A B C D E F G H I J K L M

N O P Q R S T U V W X Y Z

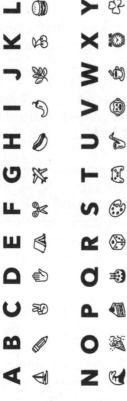

125

30

Tumbling down

My sister and I thought it would be a good idea to knock down the stone wall that stood between the patio and the grass in our garden.

I don't know how old I was when this happened - probably old enough to know that it was a really bad idea!

But we were confident. After all, the wall was cracked and parts of it had already started to fall away. **How hard could it be?**

So we began to pull down the wall - literally with our bare hands, like Marvel superheroes. At first it was satisfying. The garden would look so much better without this hideous stone wall. But after about thirty minutes, we were exhausted. We were sweating, our hands were aching, and we were hungry! We just wanted to **give up**.

What had we *done*?! Half the wall was still standing, and there were pieces of stone all over the patio.

We knew we couldn't quit. We'd get into so much trouble if our parents came home to find half a wall in the garden! We had to keep going.

So many times we wanted to give up on this mammoth task. We'd stop, rest for a bit, then carry on.

It took the entire afternoon, but eventually we pulled the whole thing down.

The garden looked beautiful. Even our parents agreed.

So often in life, when things get hard or we don't see the results we expect straight away, we just want to give up. I know - I've been there!

I want to share two Bible verses with you. The first one says: **"The LORD himself will fight for you!"** (Exodus 14:14, NLT). I've clung to this verse so many times when I've been finding life hard. It reminds me that God is with me, has my back, and wants the best for me. The second one, from Galatians 6:9 (ICB), says:

"We must not become tired of doing good. We will receive our harvest of eternal life at the right time. We must not give up!"

I want to encourage you not to give up, even when life gets hard. God is right there with you in the hard parts of life. And when God is with you, there is something wonderful on the other side of every challenge.

HEAVENLY FATHER,

Sometimes things in life feel hard and I just want to give up. Help me to remember that, no matter how hard life gets, you are with me. In Jesus' name. Amen

Word puzzle

Complete the puzzle using the words from Exodus 14:14:
"The LORD himself will fight for you!" (NLT).

Use these letters to complete the verse:

F S W R I T D Y L G E O T O I

Have you ever had to face something really hard that you couldn't do at first? Like learning all your times tables or swimming lengths at the pool? If we had all given up when we found learning to walk hard, we'd all be shuffling around on our bottoms now!

What's Up challenge

Is there something you're finding so hard right now that you want to quit?

I'm finding it hard to...

Try reminding yourself why you started in the first place, and ask God to give you the strength and motivation to carry on.

More encouragements from the Bible

- "I will praise you, LORD, with all my heart. I will tell all the miracles you have done."

  Psalm 9:1 (NLT)

- "Trust in the LORD forever, for the LORD, the LORD himself, is the Rock eternal."

  Isaiah 26:4 (NIV)

- "You will search for me. And when you search for me with all your heart, you will find me!"

  Jeremiah 29:13 (ICB)

- "'For my thoughts are not your thoughts, neither are your ways my ways,' declares the LORD. 'As the heavens are higher than the earth, so are my ways higher than your ways and my thoughts than your thoughts.'"

  Isaiah 55:8-9 (NIV)

- "So be humble under God's powerful hand. Then he will lift you up when the right time comes. Give all your worries to him, because he cares for you."

  1 Peter 5:6-7 (ICB)

- "Have I not commanded you? Be strong and courageous. Do not be afraid; do not be discouraged, for the LORD your God will be with you wherever you go."

  Joshua 1:9 (NIV)

- "So don't worry, because I am with you. Don't be afraid, because I am your God. I will make you strong and will help you. I will support you with my right hand that saves you."

  Isaiah 41:10 (ICB)

- "But the LORD said to me, 'My grace is enough for you. When you are weak, then my power is made perfect in you.' So I am very happy to brag about my weaknesses. Then Christ's power can live in me."

  2 Corinthians 12:9 (ICB)

- "Don't let anyone look down on you because you are young, but set an example for the believers in speech, in conduct, in love, in faith and in purity."

  1 Timothy 4:12 (NIV)

What's Up extra!

What might God be saying to you?
Use these pages to doodle your thoughts.

"Don't let anyone look down on you because you are young, but set an example for the believers in speech, in conduct, in love, in faith and in purity."

1 Timothy 4:12 (NIV)

Decorate the page.

134

This book is full of stories!

Do you see God working in your life or in the lives of others around you? Use this space to record YOUR stories.

Gratitude check-in!

Write five things you are grateful for.

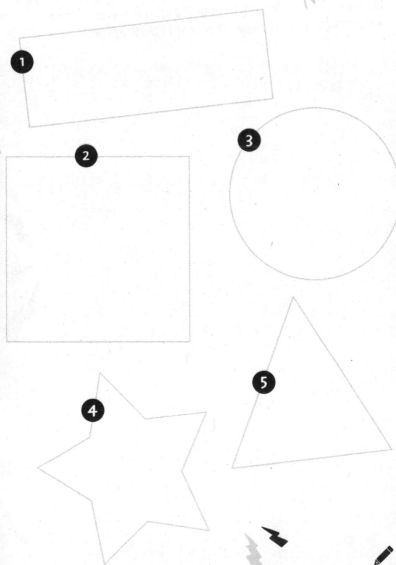

"Trust in the LORD forever, for the LORD, the LORD himself, is the Rock eternal."

Isaiah 26:4 (NIV)

✏️ Decorate the page.

Why don't you write your own prayer?

Start by telling God how awesome he is.

WOAH
He's
Awesome
_____
_____

Now thank God for something that is happening in your life.

THANK YOU
_____
_____

And say sorry for anything you've done that you shouldn't have.

SORRY
_____
_____

U can ask God anything, just don't forget to say ...

PLEASE!
_____
_____
_____
_____
_____
_____
_____

Write a prayer for someone you know.
This could be someone in your family or one of your friends.

_____

_____

_____

_____

_____

_____

Write a prayer about what's happening in the world at the moment.

_____

_____

_____

_____

_____

Index

For creative ways to pray, look inside . . .

ISBN: 9780281078479